Health AND Fitness

Healthy Food

A. R. Schaefer

Heinemann Library,
Chicago, IL

www.heinemannraintree.com
Visit our website to find out more information about Heinemann-Raintree books.

To order:
☎ Phone 888-454-2279
💻 Visit www.heinemannraintree.com to browse our catalog and order online.

Edited by Rebecca Rissman and Catherine Veitch
Designed by Kimberly R. Miracle and Betsy Wernert
Picture research by Elizabeth Alexander
Originated by Dot Gradations Ltd.
Printed in China

14 13
10 9 8 7 6 5 4

Library of Congress Cataloging-in-Publication Data

Schaefer, Adam.
  Healthy food / Adam Schaefer.
    p. cm. -- (Health and fitness)
  Includes bibliographical references and index.
  ISBN 978-1-4329-2768-4 (hc) -- ISBN 978-1-4329-2773-8 (pb)
  1. Nutrition--Juvenile literature. 2. Diet--Juvenile literature. I. Title.
  TX355.S295 2009
  613.2--dc22
                        2008052367

Acknowledgments

We would like to thank the following for permission to reproduce photographs: © Capstone Global Library Ltd. p. **12** (Tudor Photography); Alamy p. **16** (© Image Source Pink); Getty Images p. **6** (Altrendo Images); Photolibrary pp. **13** (Age Fotostock/Emilio Ereza), **19** (Rosenfeld), **20** (Foodfolio/Imagestate), **22** (Image Source), **23** (Banana Stock), **24** (Fresh Food Images/Maximilian Stock Ltd.), **25** (Comstock/Dynamic Graphics), **27** (Mark Bolton/Garden Picture Library), **28** (James Darell/Digital Vision); Rex Features pp. **8** (Image Source), **29** (Deddeda/Design Pics Inc.); Science Photo Library p. **5** (Anthony Cooper); Shutterstock pp. **4** (© Galina Barskaya), **7** (© Elena Talberg), **10** (© debr22pics), **11** (© Geanina Bechea), **14** (© emily2k), **15 & 26** (© Kiselev Andrey Valerevich), **17** (© Monkey Business Images), **18** (© Janet Hastings), **21** (© R. Gino Santa Maria); © USDA Center for Nutrition Policy & Promotion p. **9**.

Cover photograph of a girl eating an apple reproduced with permission of PunchStock (Digital Vision).

The publishers would like to thank Nicole Clark for her assistance in the preparation of this book.

Every effort has been made to contact copyright holders of any material reproduced in this book. Any omissions will be rectified in subsequent printings if notice is given to the publisher.

All the Internet addresses (URLs) given in this book were valid at the time of going to press. However, due to the dynamic nature of the Internet, some addresses may have changed, or sites may have changed or ceased to exist since publication. While the author and Publishers regret any inconvenience this may cause readers, no responsibility for any such changes can be accepted by either the author or the Publishers.

Contents

Some words are shown in bold, **like this**. You can find out what they mean by looking in the glossary.

Healthy Food

Sometimes people say that you are what you eat. The food you eat can make you healthy or unhealthy. It is your choice.

People who eat healthy food feel good.

Eating well is one part of a healthy life. We should all try to eat healthy foods and try to have a **balanced diet**.

Vegetables are a type of healthy food.

Eating Regular Meals

Your Choice:

Do you think it is a good idea to eat one very big meal? Or is it better to eat several smaller meals during the day?

Eating the right amount of food is important.

It is better to eat smaller meals throughout the day. These meals give your body the **energy** it needs throughout the whole day.

A healthy sandwich will give you energy for hours.

Balancing Your Diet

Everyone needs to eat a range of different foods to stay healthy. **Whole-grain** bread is a healthy food. But eating only bread is not healthy.

Eat foods from all of these food groups to stay healthy.

This pyramid shows the different groups of food.

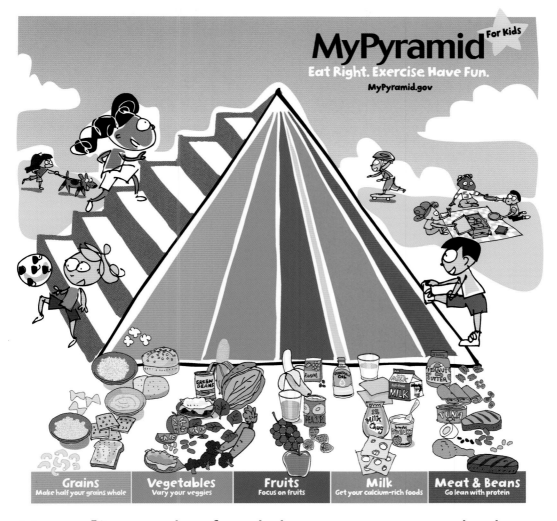

Your **diet** is the food that you eat each day. **Protein**, **grains**, vegetables, fruits, and milk are all important parts of a healthy diet.

Healthy Grains

Your Choice:

A donut has a lot of flour in it. Flour is made from **grains**. Is eating a donut a good way to get grains in your **diet**?

A lot of people like donuts, but are they healthy?

Donuts are not a very healthy food. They are made with grains, but also with a lot of sugar and **fat**. Healthy grains include **whole-grain** bread and pasta, brown rice, and corn tortillas.

Try to eat healthy grains a few times each day.

Healthy Fruits

Fruit contains **vitamins** that are healthy for you.

Fruit is great for your body. Fresh fruits are the best for your health. Fresh fruits have not been cooked and look like they have just been picked.

Apples, oranges, bananas, pears, and berries all taste good fresh. Canned, dried, and frozen fruits are also healthy.

Food like fruit candies, ice cream, and cakes should not be a part of a healthy **diet** each day.

Healthy Vegetables

Your Choice:

You know vegetables are healthy. You can eat a fresh salad or french fries. Which one is a better choice?

French fries are made from potatoes, but are they healthy?

Fresh vegetables are better for your health than **fried** foods. A salad with fresh spinach, lettuce, tomatoes, and other vegetables is very healthy. Cooked vegetables, like corn, baked potatoes, and broccoli are healthy also.

Eat uncooked vegetables to get the most **nutrients**.

Healthy Milk Foods

Milk foods are an important part of a good **diet**. Yogurt and cheese are made from milk. These foods help your bones grow strong.

Dairy products like these are good for your teeth and bones.

There is cheese on these nachos, but it is not a very healthy meal.

Yogurt and milk are healthy dairy foods. A little cheese and butter is fine, but you should not eat too much as they contain a lot of **fat**. Ice cream is a dairy food but it has too much fat and sugar to be healthy every day.

Healthy Proteins

Your Choice:

There is **protein** in chicken. Is **fried** chicken a healthy way to eat protein?

Meats like chicken have a lot of protein.

Fried foods are mostly unhealthy. Small amounts of **grilled** meat, chicken, and fish are much healthier. There is also a lot of healthy protein in nuts and beans.

Protein helps build muscles in your body.

Fats

Healthy fats are an important part of our diet.

Fats help keep our skin and other **organs** healthy. But some fats are healthier choices than others. Healthy fats come from fruits, nuts, and vegetables, such as avocados and corn.

Try to limit the food you eat that is high in **animal fat**, such as hamburgers and **fried** meat. These foods are full of unhealthy fats.

Most fast food is high in unhealthy fats.

Water and Other Liquids

Your Choice:

We know that we need to drink water to live. Sodas are mostly water. Are sodas a good way to drink water?

Avoid drinks with a lot of sugar and chemicals.

Drink several glasses of water each day.

While sodas have water in them, other ingredients make these drinks unhealthy, such as sugar and chemicals. The best drink is plain water. Fruit juice is nice to drink with meals but it also contains a lot of sugar so it is best not to drink too much.

Unhealthy Food

Your Choice:

Some foods, such as hamburgers and ice cream, are bad for our health. Is it ever alright to eat those things?

Do not eat too much food with lots of sugar and fat.

Eating unhealthy foods, such as cakes, cookies, and chips does not help our bodies to grow and stay well. But if we eat healthy food most of the time, an occasional treat is alright and can be fun.

A little ice cream or candy is fine at a special time, such as a birthday party.

Fresh Food Is Fantastic

For most foods, fresh is best. Fresh fruits and vegetables have more **nutrients** in them than food that has been kept in plastic packages or cans.

Fresh fruit looks good, too.

Moldy or bad-smelling food is not good for us and can make us sick. It is a good idea to check bread and cheese for **mold**. Make sure that fruit and vegetables are firm and ripe.

Moldy food can make you sick and it smells and looks unhealthy.

Healthy Habits for Life

It is easier to get into good eating **habits** when you are around other people who have good habits. Ask your family and friends to start eating healthily with you.

A meal or snack always tastes better when you share it.

Healthy habits can last your whole life.

It is never too late or too early to start eating well. Even people who have been unhealthy for years feel better when they start to eat well. Getting into good habits while you are young will start a lifetime of healthy eating.

Glossary

animal fat part of an animal that is not very healthy for humans to eat

balanced diet diet that has a mix of different foods. Includes proteins, grains, vegetables, fruits, and milk.

diet what you usually eat and drink

energy power needed for your body to work and stay alive

fat oil found in some food

fried cooked in oil or another fat

grain seed from a cereal plant, such as wheat or corn

grill cook food by putting it close to something hot

habit thing you do often

mold kind of organism that grows on rotten things

nutrient substance (such as a vitamin or protein) that people need to grow and stay healthy

organ part inside your body that does certain jobs

protein part of some food that helps the body to grow and stay healthy

vitamin part of some food that helps the body to grow and stay healthy

whole-grain grain such as oats, wheat, corn, or rice that have all or most of their natural fiber and nutrients

Find Out More

Books to Read

Evers, Connie Liakos. *Good For You!* New York: Disney Learning, 2006.

Giddens, Sandra. *Making Smart Choices About Food, Nutrition, and Lifestyle.* New York: Rosen Pub., 2008.

Goulding, Sylvia. *Healthy Eating.* Vero Beach, Fla.: Rourke Publishing, 2005.

Gray, Shirley W. *Eating for Good Health.* Chanhassen, Minn.: Child's World, 2004.

Schaefer, Lola. *Food Groups.* Chicago: Heinemann Library, 2009.

Senker, Cath. *Healthy Eating.* New York: PowerKids Press, 2008.

Websites

http://kidshealth.org/kid/stay_healthy/food/pyramid.html
Learn how to eat a balanced diet with the Food Guide Pyramid.

Index